An Educational Activity/Colo

SHARK MAZES

Created by
Peter M. Spizzirri

This Is An Educational/Activity Coloring Book of SHARK MAZES• Published by SPIZZIRRI PUBLISHING, INC., P.O. BOX 9397, RAPID CITY, SOUTH DAKOTA 57709.
Printed in U.S.A.

The Sharks in This Book Are Different Sizes

Shark Name	Length
Black Tip Shark	8 ft.
Blue Shark	9 ft.
Bull Shark	9 ft.
Frill Shark	4 ft.
Gray Nurse Shark	15 ft.
Great White Shark	18 ft.
Mako Shark	6 to 12 ft.
Nurse Shark	6 ft.
Porbeagle Shark	8 ft
Port Jackson Shark	4 ft.
Sand Tiger Shark	10 ft.

Shark Name	Length
Six-Gilled Shark	17 ft.
Soupfin Shark	6 ft.
Spiny Dogfish Shark	4 ft.
Swell Shark	5 ft.
Thresher Shark	15 ft.
Tiger Shark	15 ft.
Whale Shark	40 ft.
Whaler Shark	12 ft.
White Tip Shark	10 ft.
Zebra Shark	11 ft.

Mako Shark

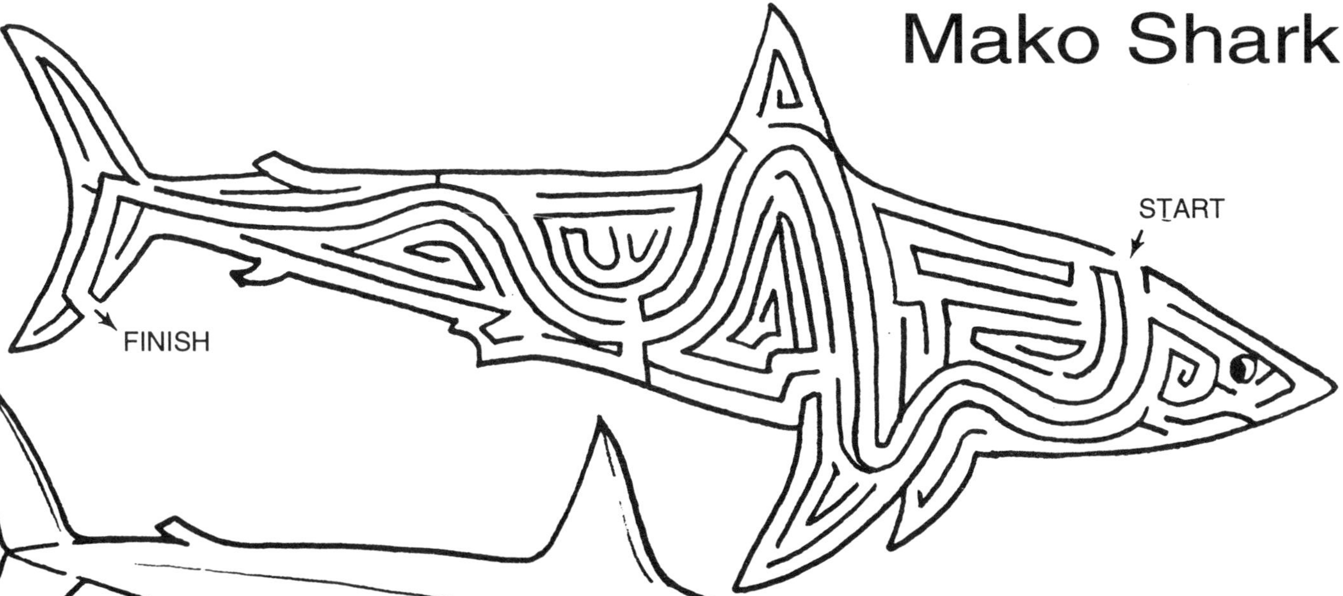

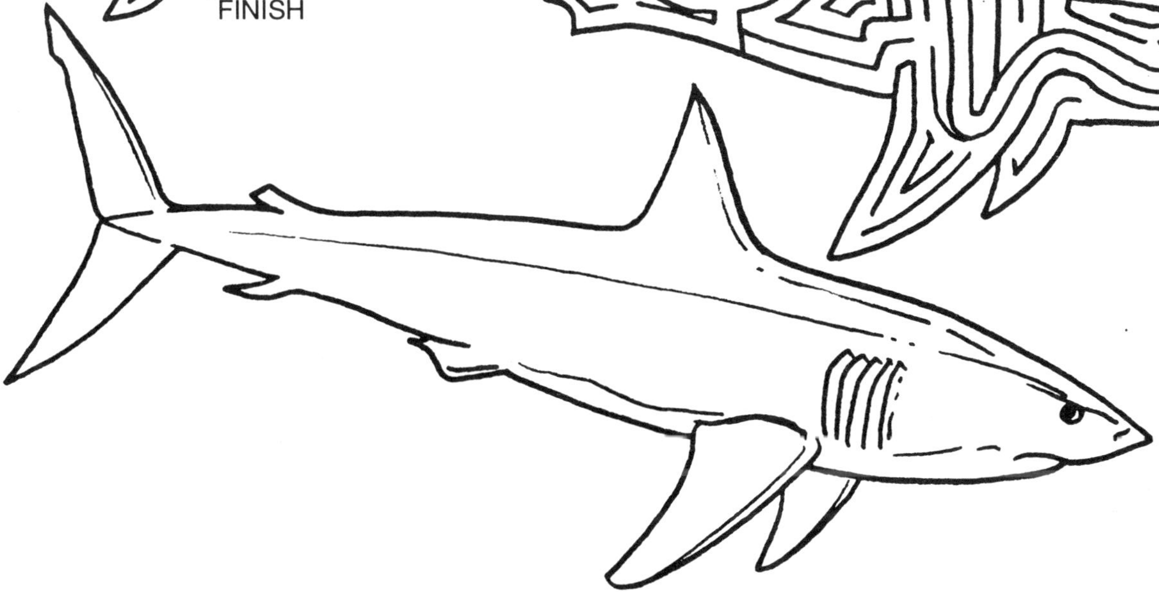

Complete the MAZE. Draw a line from START to FINISH, without crossing any black lines.

Whitetip Shark

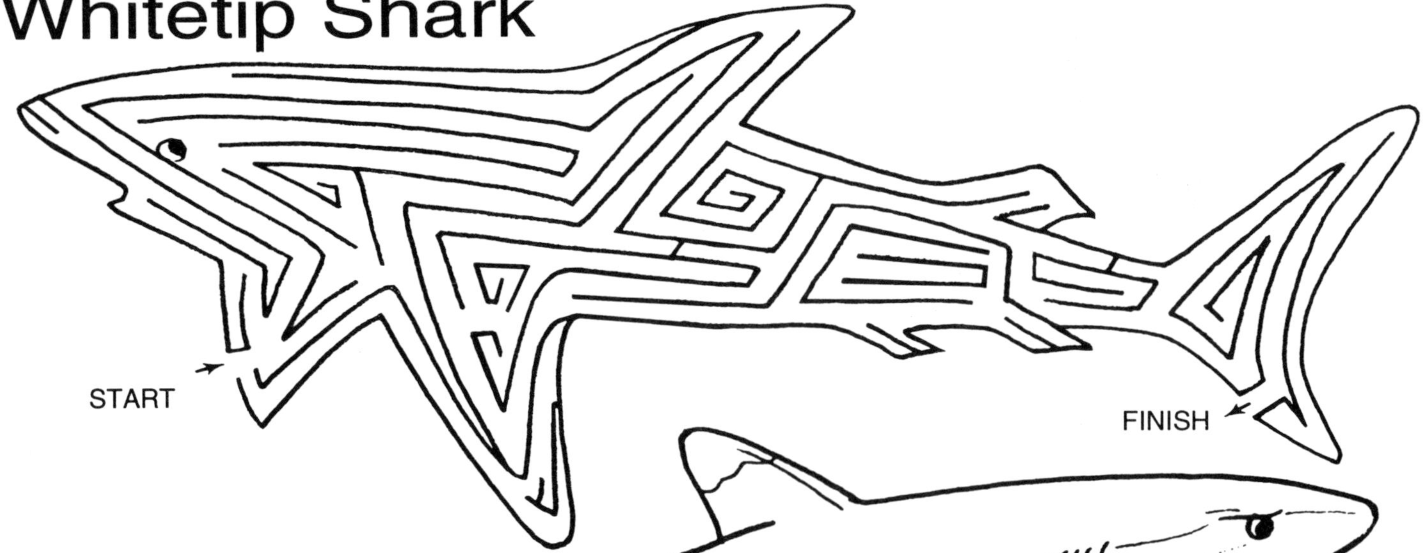

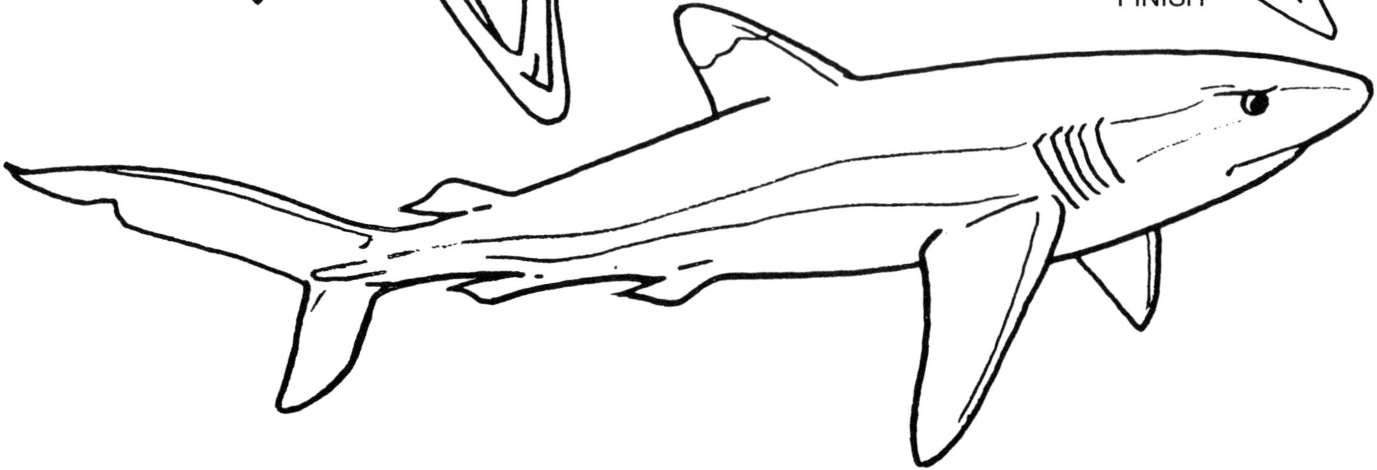

Complete the MAZE. Draw a line from START to FINISH, without crossing any black lines.

Sand Tiger Shark

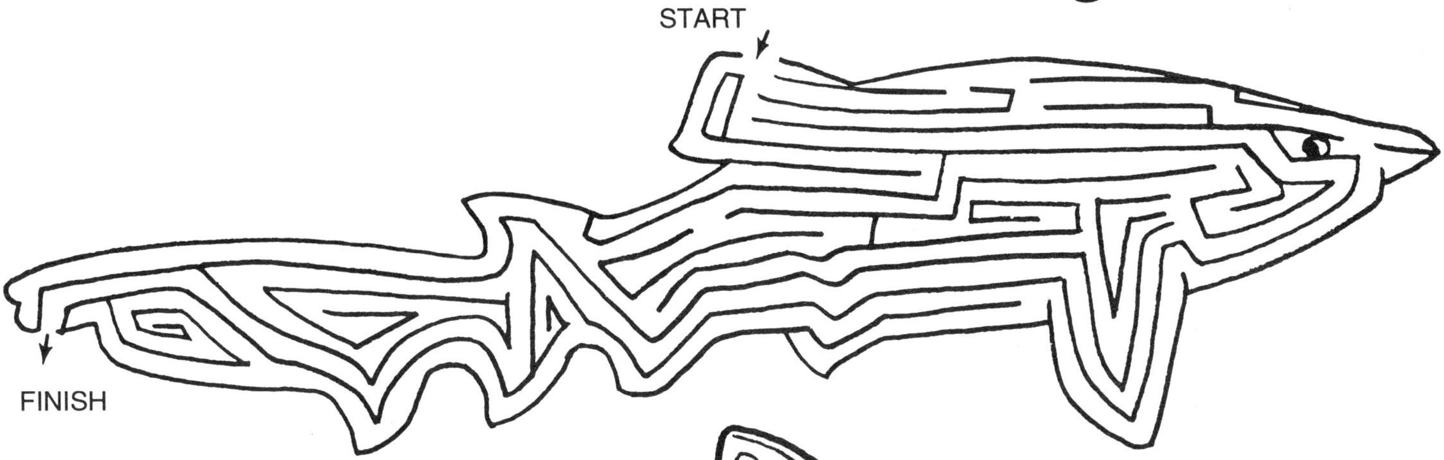

Complete the MAZE. Draw a line from START to FINISH, without crossing any black lines.

Soupfin Shark

 Complete the MAZE. Draw a line from START to FINISH, without crossing any black lines.

Thresher Shark

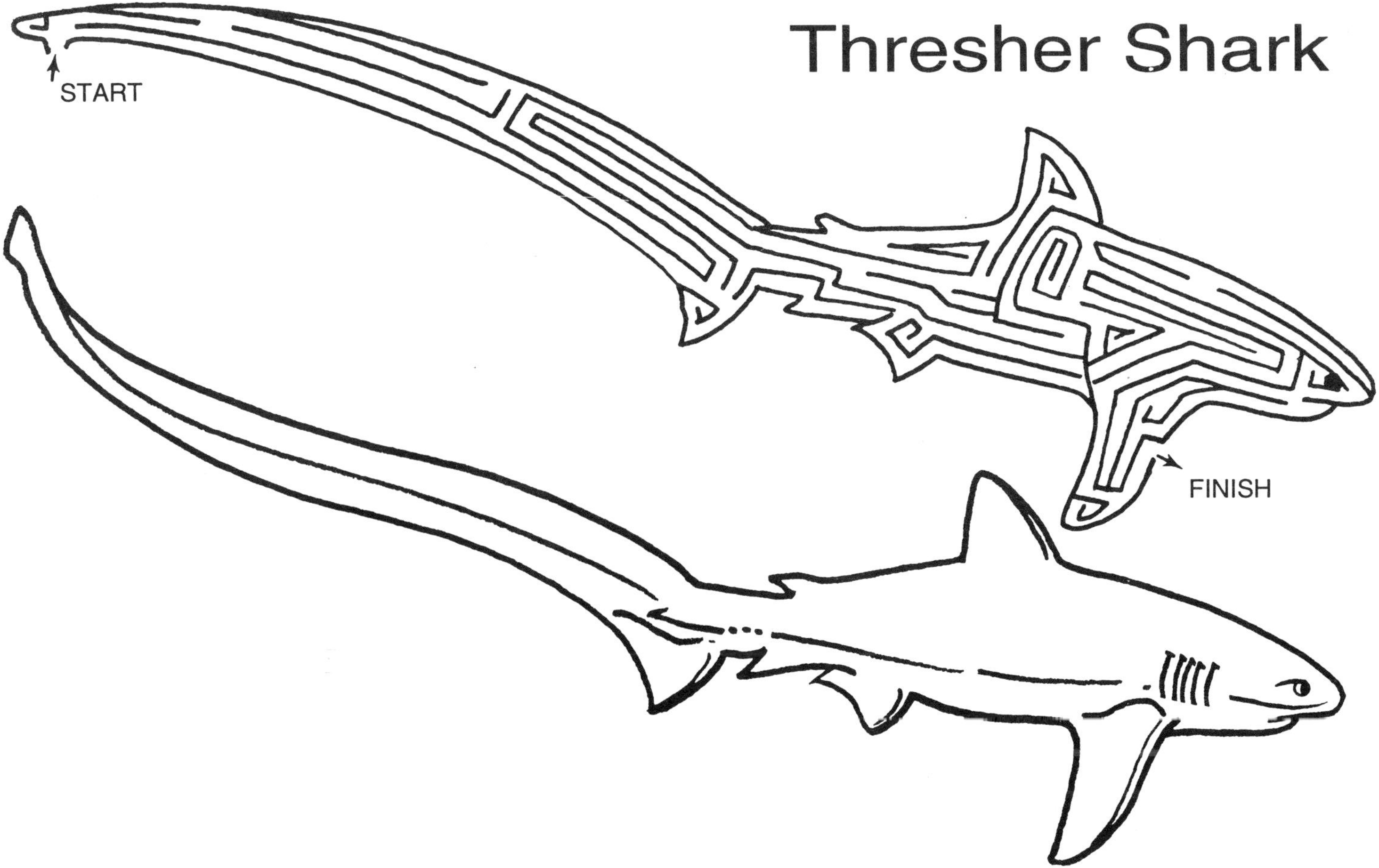

Complete the MAZE. Draw a line from START to FINISH, without crossing any black lines.

Six-Gilled Shark

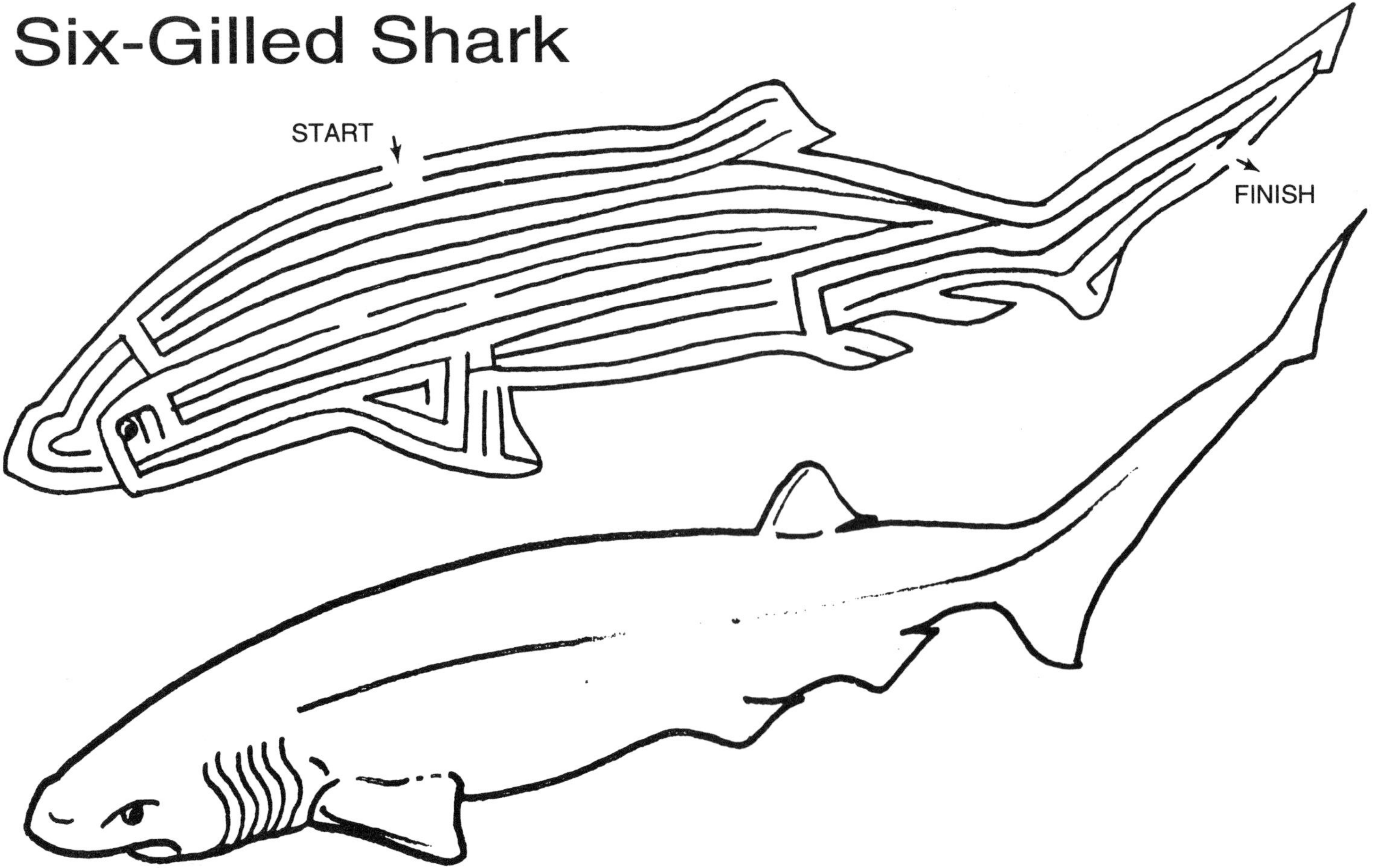

 Complete the MAZE. Draw a line from START to FINISH, without crossing any black lines.

Bull Shark

Complete the MAZE. Draw a line from START to FINISH, without crossing any black lines.

Whale Shark

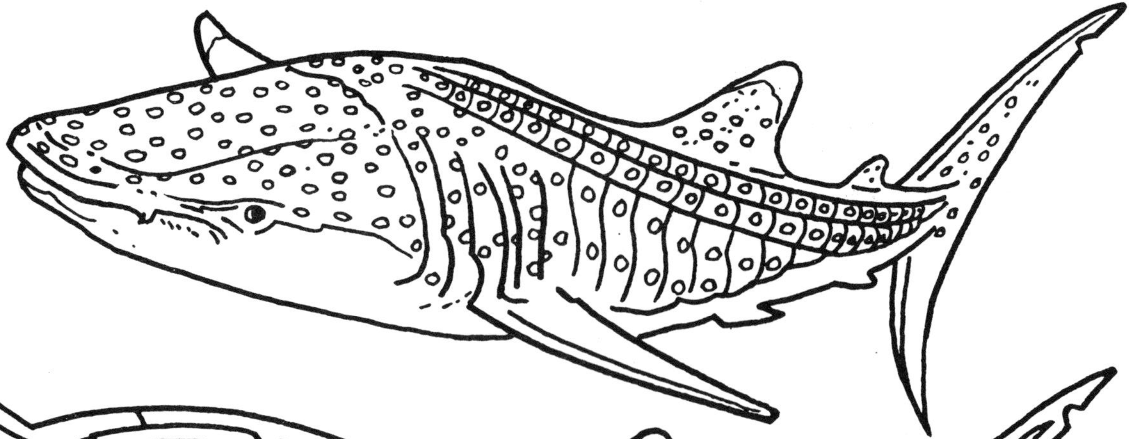

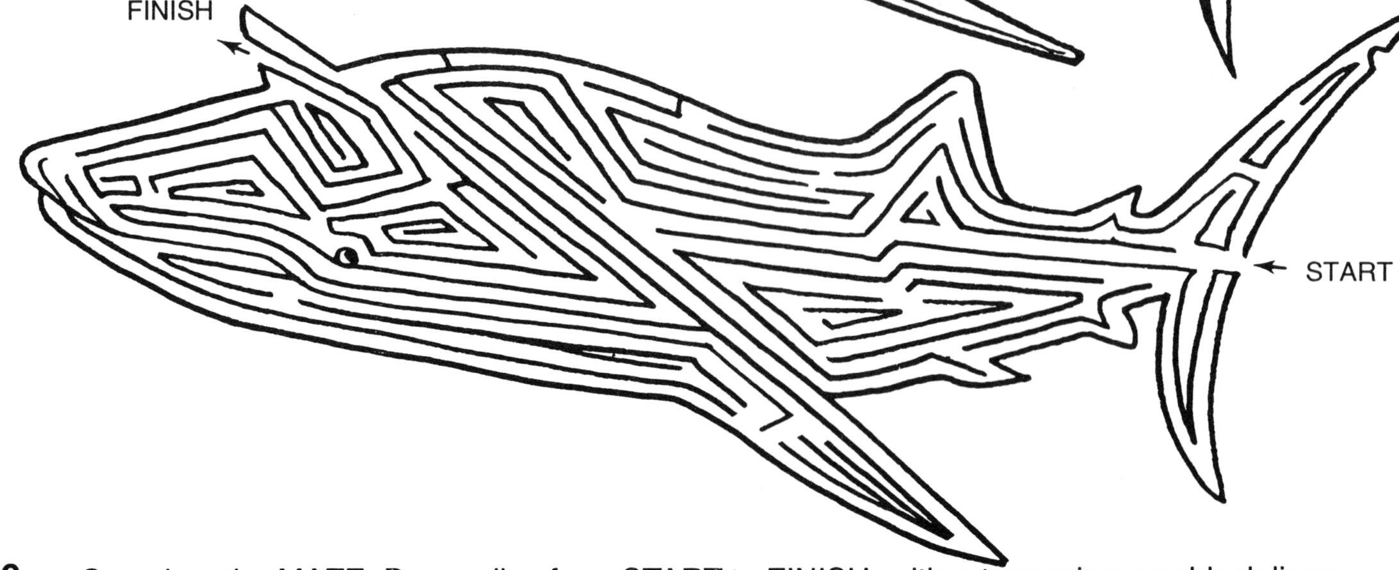

 Complete the MAZE. Draw a line from START to FINISH, without crossing any black lines.

Nurse Shark

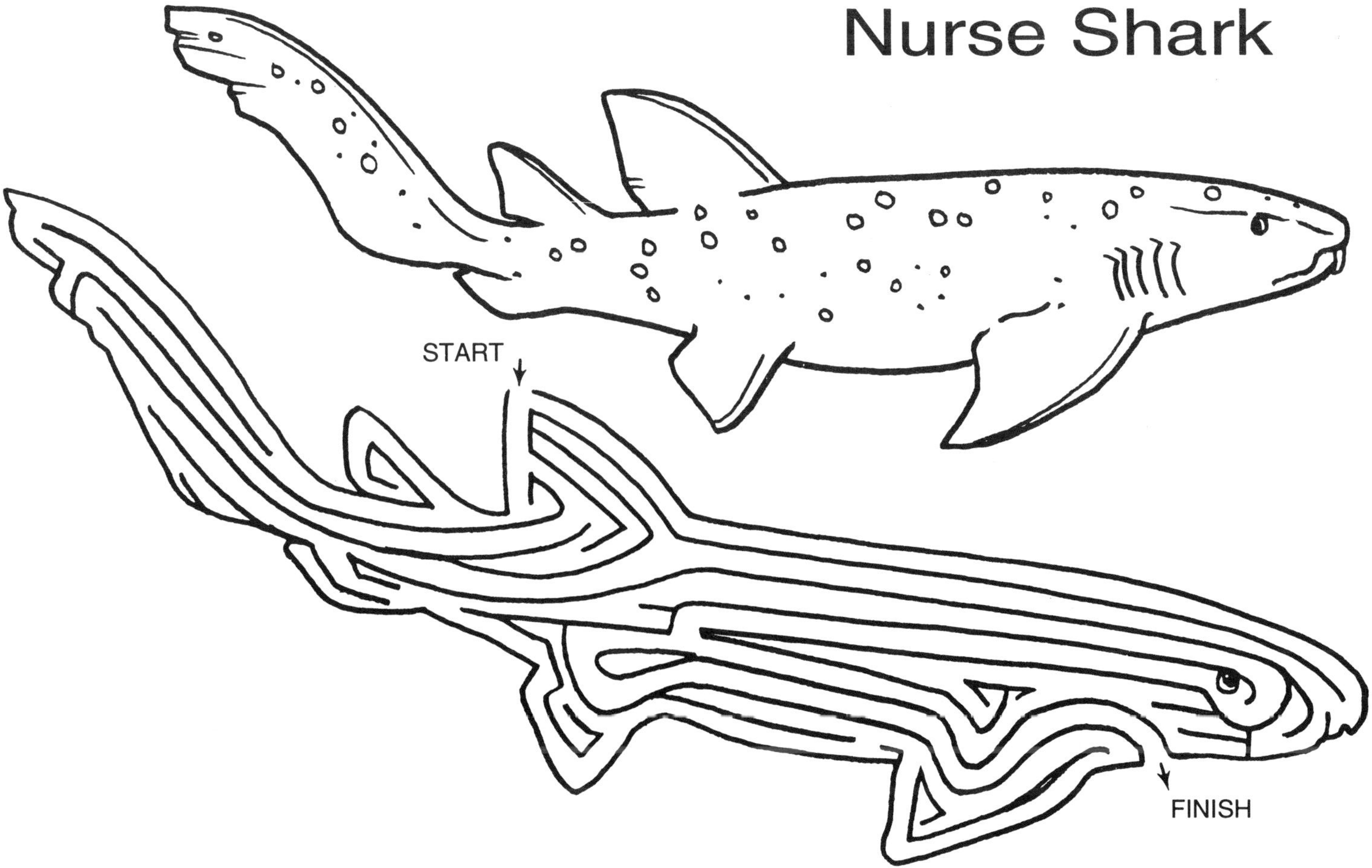

Complete the MAZE. Draw a line from START to FINISH, without crossing any black lines.

Whaler Shark

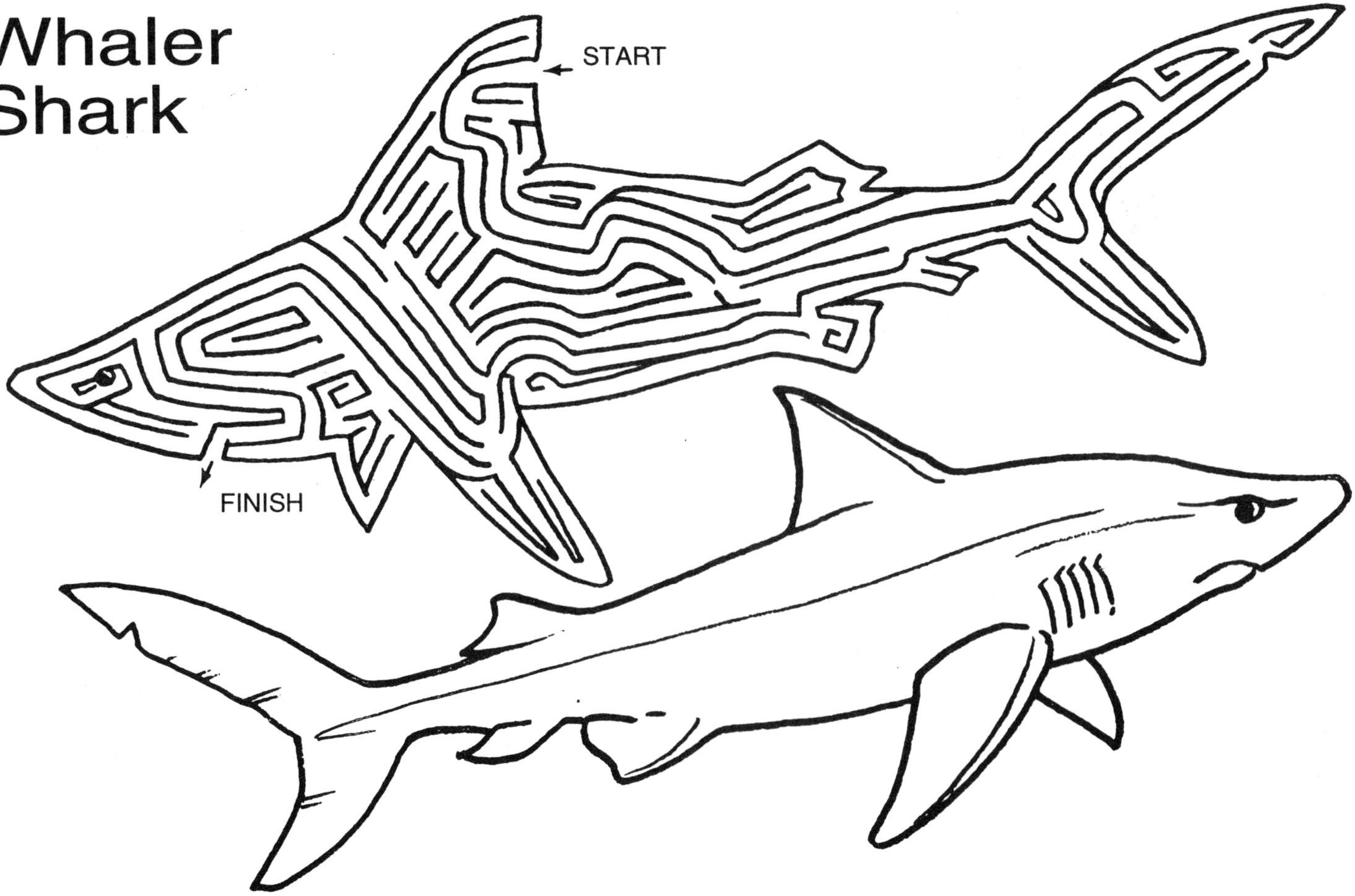

 Complete the MAZE. Draw a line from START to FINISH, without crossing any black lines.

Gray Nurse Shark

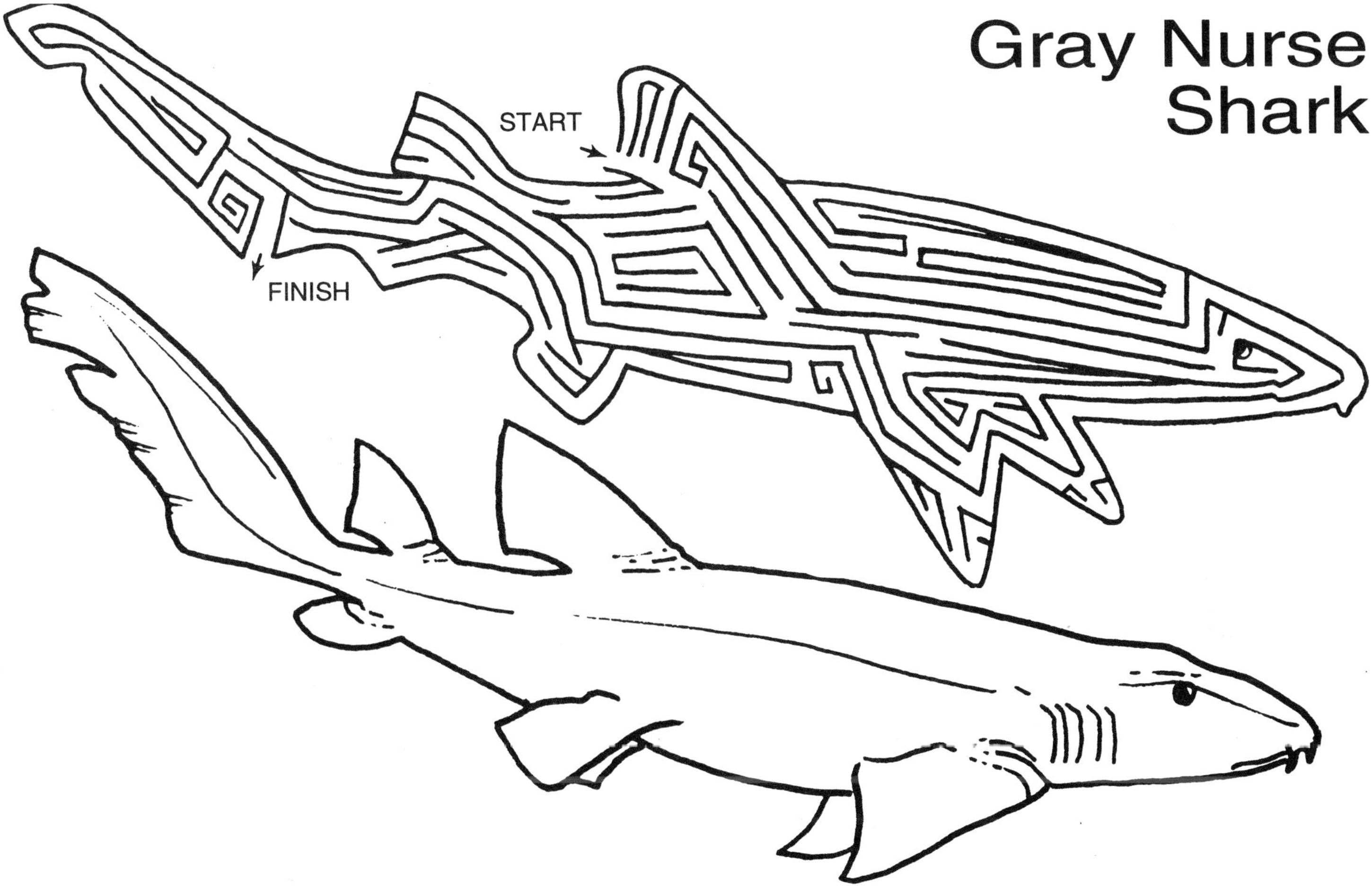

Complete the MAZE. Draw a line from START to FINISH, without crossing any black lines.

Spiny Dogfish Shark

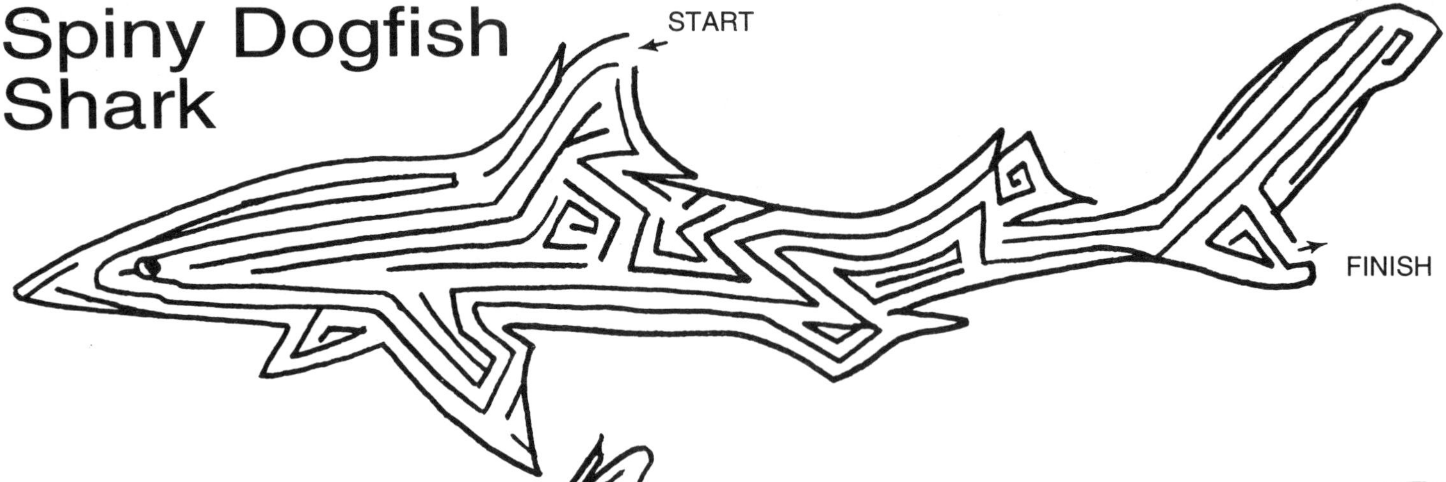

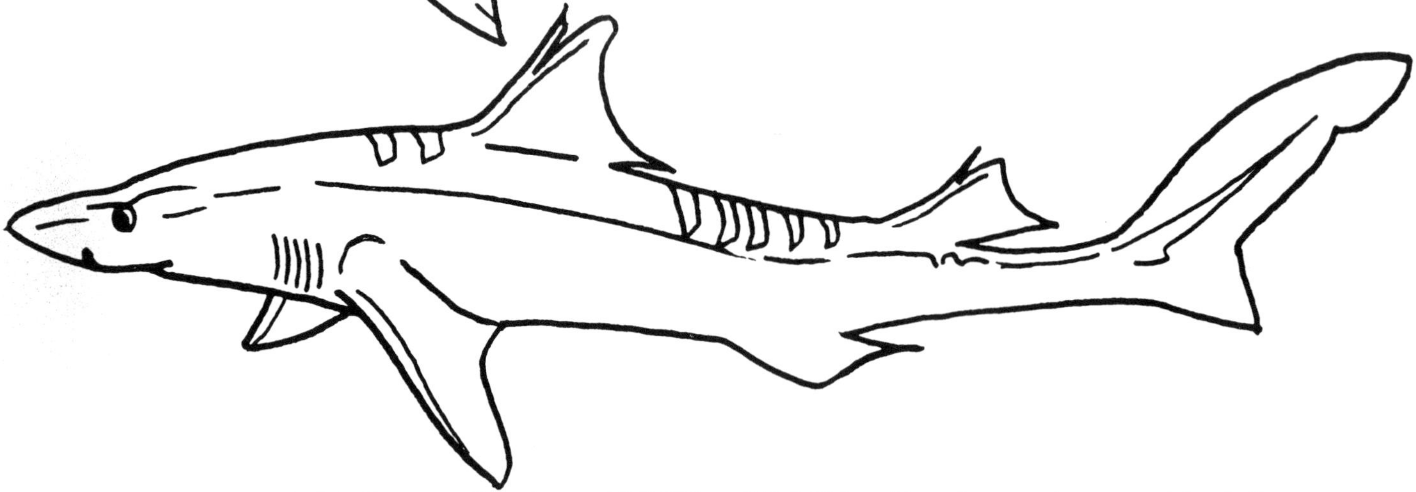

 Complete the MAZE. Draw a line from START to FINISH, without crossing any black lines.

Blue Shark

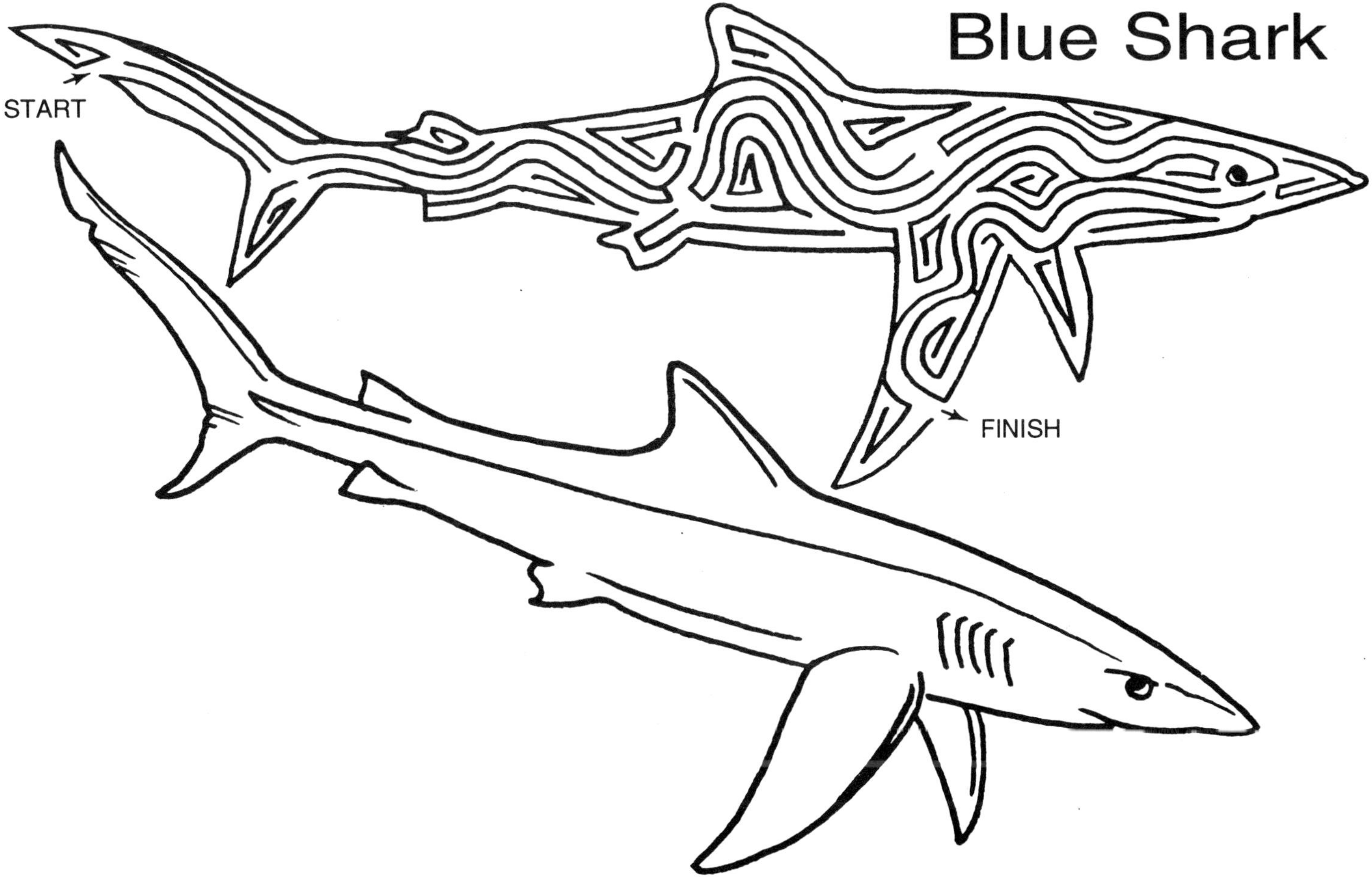

Complete the MAZE. Draw a line from START to FINISH, without crossing any black lines.

Tiger Shark

 Complete the MAZE. Draw a line from START to FINISH, without crossing any black lines.

Zebra Shark

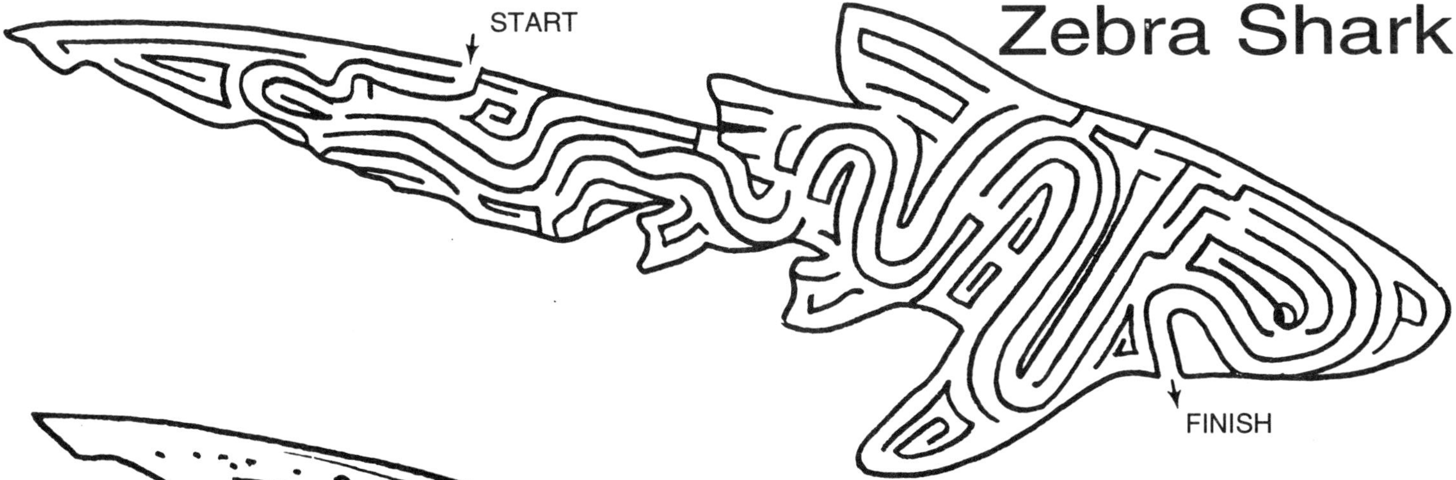

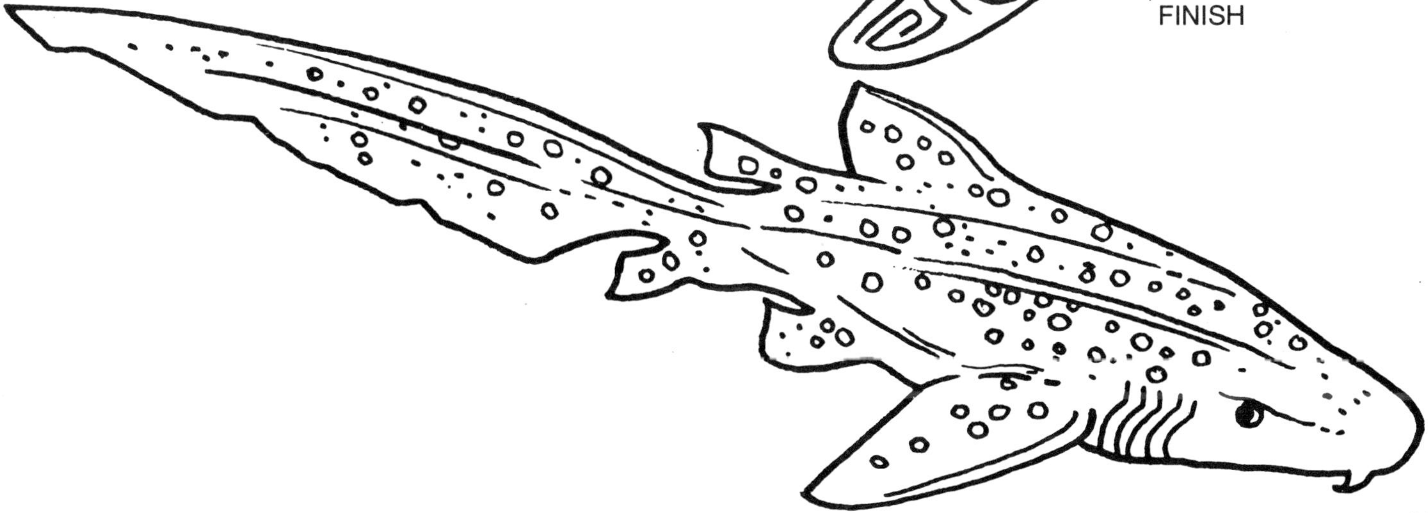

Complete the MAZE. Draw a line from START to FINISH, without crossing any black lines.

Porbeagle Shark

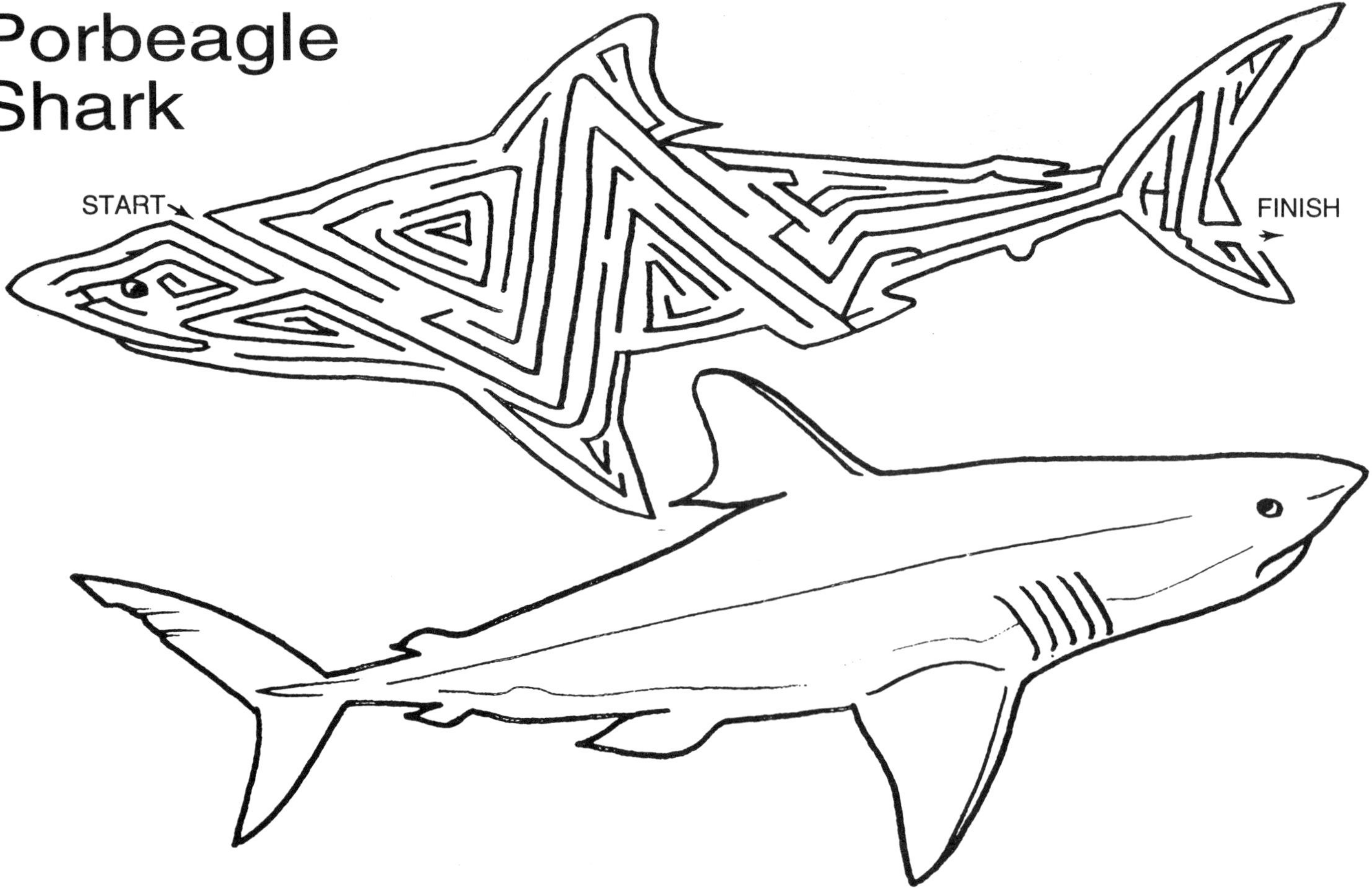

 Complete the MAZE. Draw a line from START to FINISH, without crossing any black lines.

Black Tip Shark

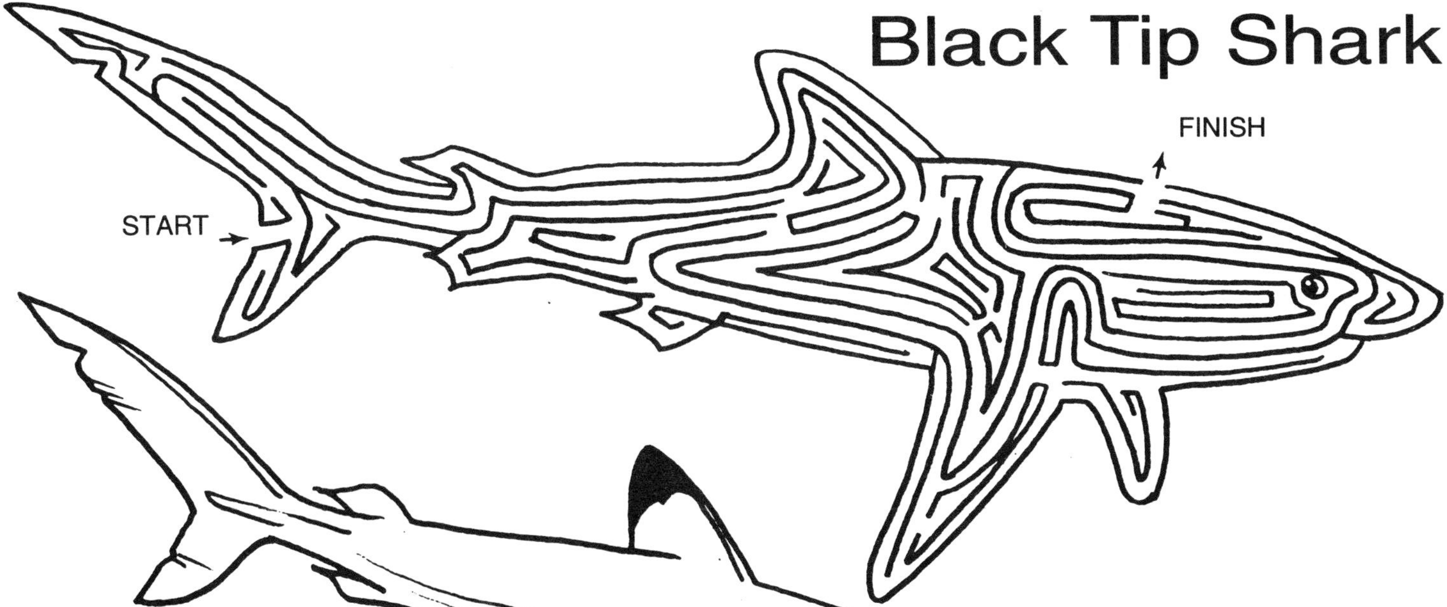

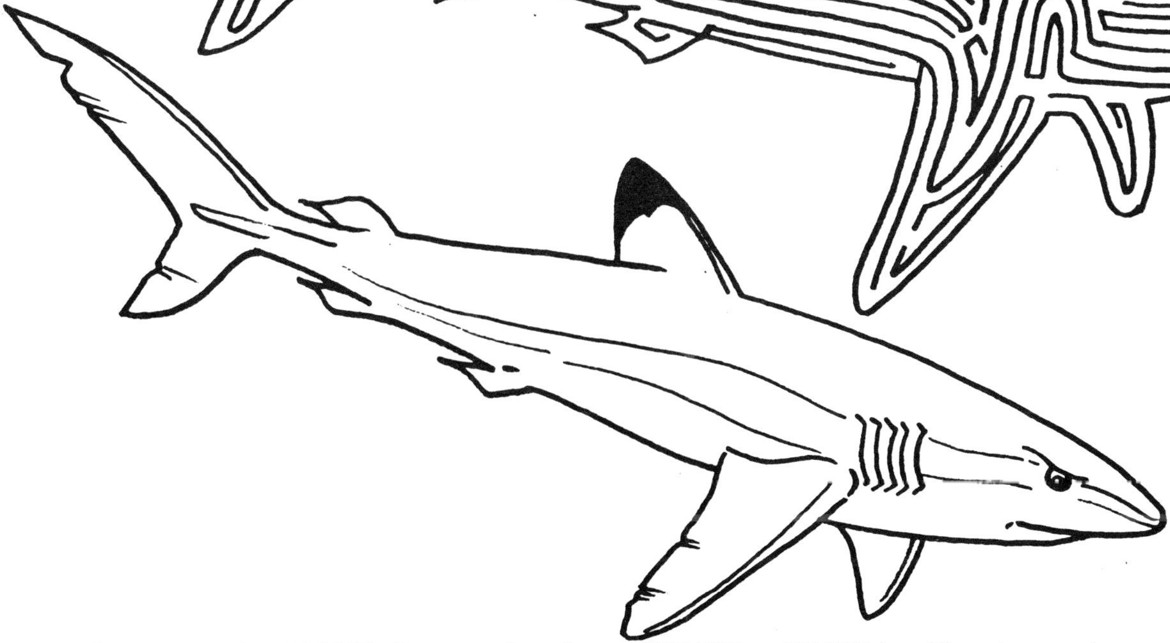

Complete the MAZE. Draw a line from START to FINISH, without crossing any black lines.

Swell Shark

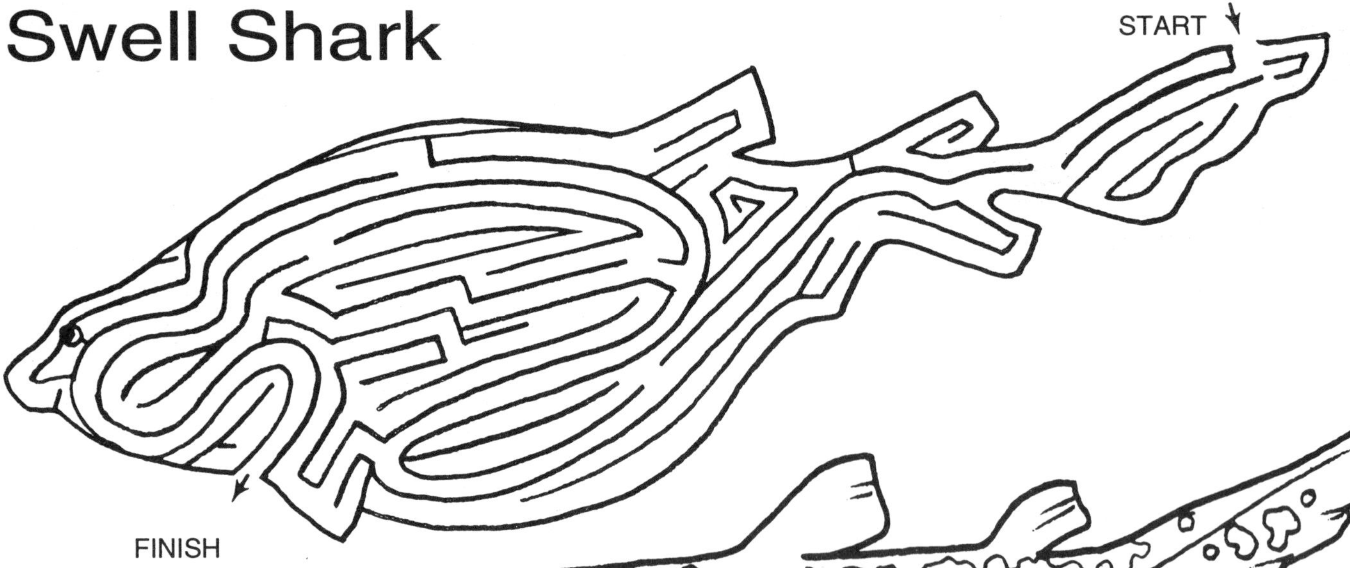

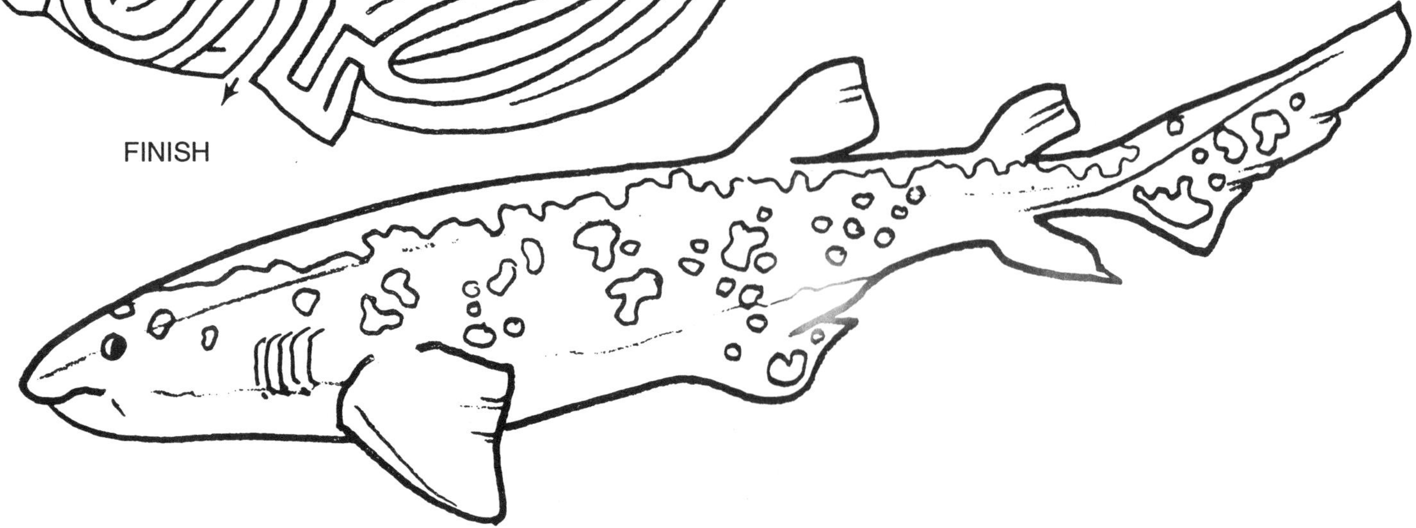

 Complete the MAZE. Draw a line from START to FINISH, without crossing any black lines.

Frill Shark

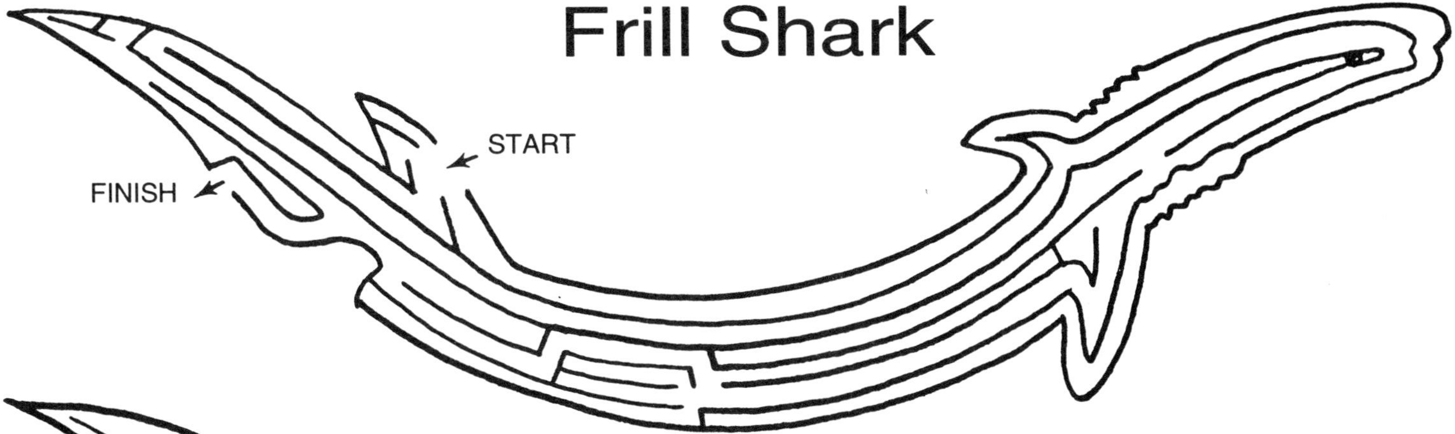

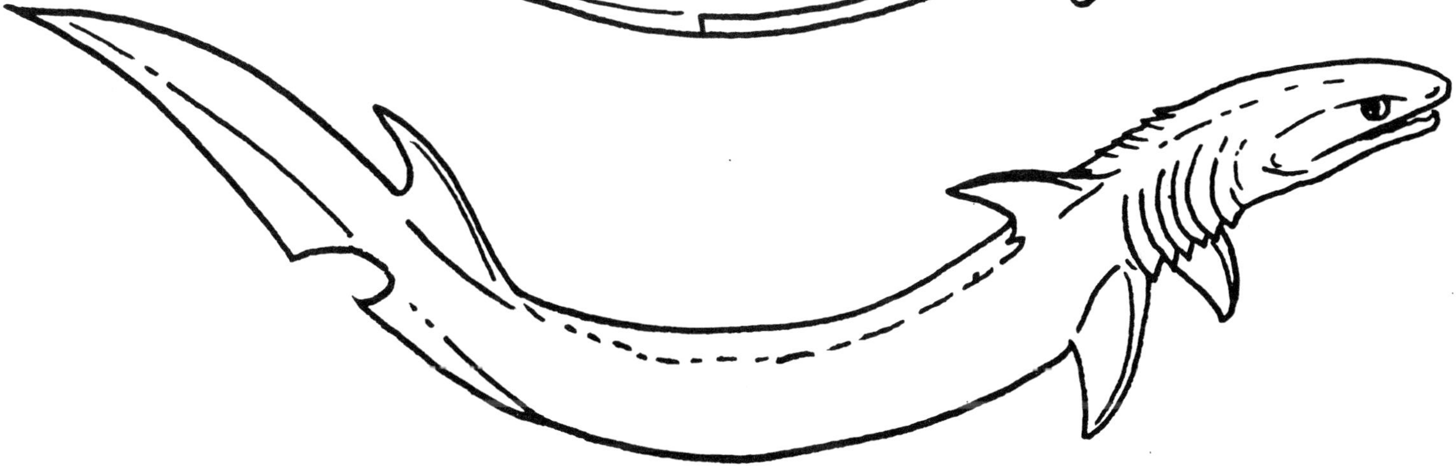

Complete the MAZE. Draw a line from START to FINISH, without crossing any black lines.

Great White Shark

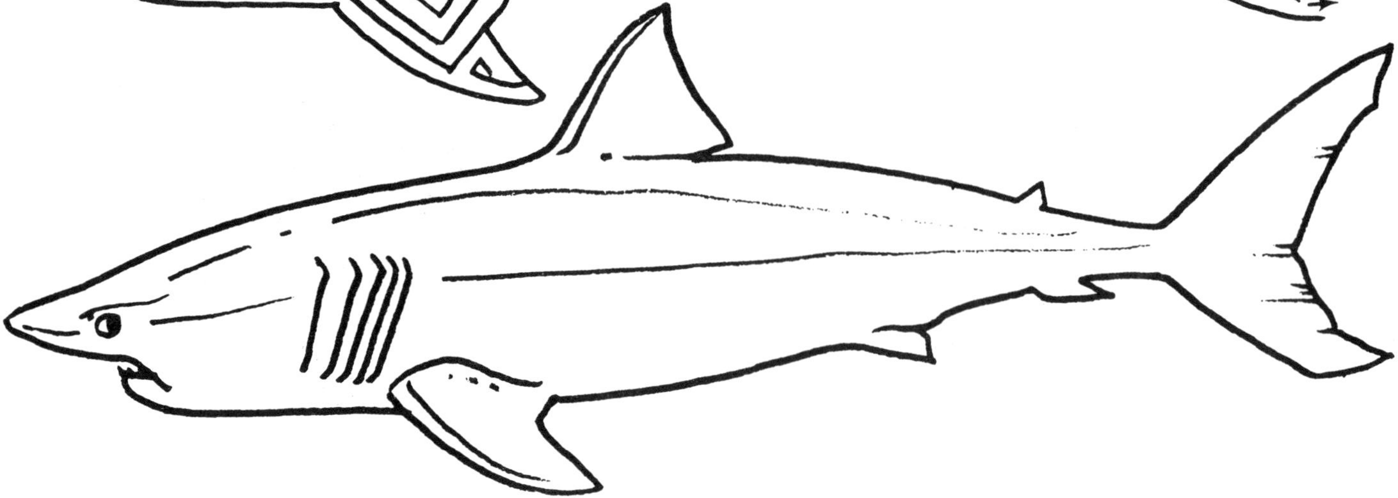

Complete the MAZE. Draw a line from START to FINISH, without crossing any black lines.

Port Jackson Shark

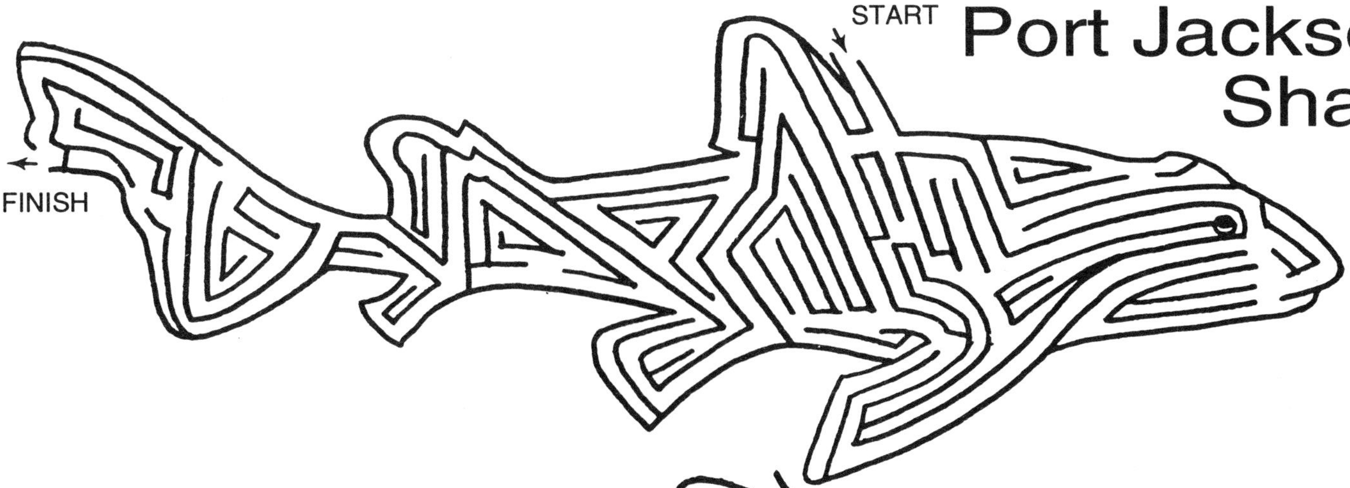

Complete the MAZE. Draw a line from START to FINISH, without crossing any black lines.

OTHER CHILDREN'S BOOKS CREATED BY SPIZZIRRI PUBLISHING

ISBN (INTERNATIONAL STANDARD BOOK NUMBER) PREFIX ON ALL SPIZZIRRI BOOKS IS: 0-86545-

EDUCATIONAL READ AND COLOR BOOKS

ILLUSTRATIONS AND TEXT
SIZE: 8 1/2" X 11"

AIRCRAFT
ANIMAL ALPHABET
ANIMAL F. CALENDAR
ANIMAL GIANTS
ATLANTIC FISH
AUTOMOBILES
BIRDS
CALIFORNIA INDIANS
CALIFORNIA MISSIONS
CATS
CATS OF THE WILD
CAVE MAN
COLONIES
COMETS
Count/Color DINOSAURS
COWBOYS
DEEP-SEA FISH
DINOSAURS
DINOSAURS OF PREY
DOGS
DOGS OF THE WILD
DOLLS
DOLPHINS
EAGLES
ENDANGERED BIRDS
Endang'd Mam'ls-AFRICA
Endang'd Mam'ls- ASIA & CHINA
Endang'd Mam'ls-SO. AMERICA
ENDANGERED SPECIES
ESKIMOS
FARM ANIMALS
FISH
HORSES
KACHINA DOLLS
LAUTREC POSTERS
MAMMALS
MARINE MAMMALS
MARSUPIALS
NORTHEAST INDIANS
NORTHWEST INDIANS
PACIFIC FISH
PALEOZOIC LIFE
PENGUINS
PICTURE CROSSWORDS
PICTURE DICTIONARY
PIONEERS
PLAINS INDIANS
PLANETS
POISONOUS SNAKES
Prehist. BIRDS
Prehist. FISH
Prehist. MAMMALS
Prehist. SEA LIFE
PRIMATES
RAIN FOREST BIRDS
RAIN FOREST RIVER LIFE
RAIN FOREST TREE LIFE
REPTILES
ROCKETS
SATELLITES
SHARKS
SHIPS
SHUTTLE CRAFT
SOUTHEAST INDIANS
SOUTHWEST INDIANS
SPACE CRAFT
SPACE EXPLORERS
STATE BIRDS
STATE FLOWERS
TEXAS
TRANSPORTATION
TRUCKS
WHALES

SILHOUETTE ART BOOKS

8 1/2 x 11" Reproducible

CHRISTMAS
CIRCUS
DINOSAURS
FARM ANIMALS
OCEAN LIFE
ZOO ANIMALS

EDUCATIONAL ACTIVITY BOOKS

SIZE: 5 1/2 x 8 1/2"

Alphabet Dot-to-dot PETS
Alphabet Dot-to-dot ZOO ANIMALS
BIRD MAZES
BUTTERFLY MAZES
DINOSAUR MAZES
Dot-to-dot DINOSAURS
Dot-to-dot FISH
Dot-to-dot REPTILES
Dot-to-dot WHALES
FARM MAZES
FISH MAZES
FLOWER MAZES
MAMMAL MAZES
SHARK MAZES
SHELL MAZES
TREE MAZES
TURTLE MAZES
ZOO MAZES

EARLY LEARNING WORKBOOKS

SIZE: 8 1/2 x 11"

ALPHABET PICTURES
COMPLETE THE WORDS
COUNTING DINOSAURS
Dot to dot ALPHABET
Dot to dot NUMBERS
FIRST ADDITION
FIRST ALPHABET
FIRST NUMBERS
FIRST SUBTRACTION
MAKE A CALENDAR
MAKING WORDS
MAZE PUZZLES
NUMBERS and COLORS
PICTURE CROSSWORDS
PICTURE DICTIONARY
SHAPES, ART & COLORS
THEY GO TOGETHER
TRIANGLE PICTURES
WORD HUNT PUZZLES
WORDS IN WORDS

Educational FACTS and FUN Books

SIZE: 5 1/2 X 8 1/2"

ANIMAL LEAPS
ANIMAL SPEEDS
ANIMALS THAT LAY EGGS
ANIMALS WITH LONG NECKS
ANIMALS WITH LONG TAILS
BIRD SPEEDS
FOOTPRINTS OF BIRDS
INSECT HUNTERS
MAMMAL FOOTPRINTS
POISONOUS ANIMALS
SKATES AND RAYS
SMALL MAMMALS